FUN WITH Outer Space

FUN WITH Outer Space

A Big Activity Book for Kids about Our Incredible Universe

EMILY GREENHALGH

ILLUSTRATED BY CANDELA FERRÁNDEZ

Z KIDS • NEW YORK

Copyright © 2024 by Penguin Random House LLC

All rights reserved.
Published in the United States by Z Kids, an imprint of Zeitgeist™,
a division of Penguin Random House LLC, New York.
zeitgeistpublishing.com

Zeitgeist™ is a trademark of Penguin Random House LLC.

ISBN: 9780593689875

Illustrations by Candela Ferrández

Book design by Aimee Fleck

Illustrator photograph © by Artur Laperla

Manufactured in China

1st Printing

TO MIKE, ZU, DAVID, AND ANYONE WHO HAS EVER WISHED ON A SHOOTING STAR

Contents

WELCOME TO OUTER SPACE! 8
THE SOLAR SYSTEM 10

THE BIG PICTURE

The Universe 14

The Big Bang 16

Atmosphere 18

Gravity 20

Speed of Light 22

The Solar System 24

Orbits 26

The Sun 28

The Moon 30

Moon Phases 32

Solar and Lunar Eclipses 34

The Planets 36

Mercury 38

Venus 40

Earth 42

Mars 44

Jupiter 46

Saturn 48

Uranus 50

Neptune 52

Dwarf Planets 54

Pluto 56

Kuiper Belt 58

Asteroids and the Asteroid Belt 60

THE SHOW IN THE SKY

Stars 64

Life of a Star 72

The Milky Way 80

Constellations 66

Supernovas 74

Comets 82

Nebulas 68

Black Holes 76

Meteoroids, Meteors, and Meteorites 84

Star Clusters 70

Galaxies 78

OUR PLACE IN SPACE

Satellites 88

Astronauts 100

International Space Station 110

Rockets 90

Spacesuits 102

Telescopes 112

Rovers 92

Living and Working in Space 104

Aliens 114

Space Probes 94

Moon Missions 106

UFOs 116

Spaceplanes 96

Mars Missions 108

Space Tourism 118

Space Explorers 98

ANSWER KEY 120

Welcome to Outer Space!

Have you ever looked up at the night sky, stared at the stars, and wondered what else is up there? You're not the only one. Since humans have existed, people have looked up at the night sky and tried to imagine what lies beyond what they can see—and there's a lot! Planet Earth is part of a system of eight planets—Mercury, Venus, Earth, Mars, Jupiter, Saturn, Uranus, and Neptune—all revolving around the sun, a star named Sol. That's why we call it the *sola*r system. We're part of a galaxy called the Milky Way, which is made up of billions of other stars, all with systems of planets. There are *billions* of galaxies like ours in the universe. Space is *that* big!

In fact, there are so many stars that if you counted all the sand on Earth, there would be nearly 10,000 stars for each grain of sand. And there's more out there in space than just stars and planets. Moons revolve around planets. In our solar system, Mercury and Venus are the only planets without moons and Earth is the only planet with just one. There are giant gas clouds called nebulas that form when a star is born and black holes so strong that even light is pulled into them.

Since space is so big, there's a lot we can't see from Earth. Scientists have sent out giant machines called satellites with cameras to take pictures and help us understand how big space is. (Did you know our universe is getting bigger every year, but scientists aren't sure how big it actually is?) They've learned that there's a lot about space we don't know yet, and there's more to explore than we could ever imagine.

With the three parts of this book—the Big Picture, the Show in the Sky, and Our Place in Space—you'll take off on a galactic journey full of fun activities like word searches and mazes and spacewalk through a starfield of fun facts. Are you ready to explore the universe? Put on your space suit and strap into your rocket—it's time to blast off!

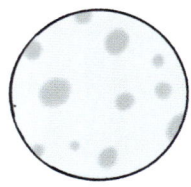

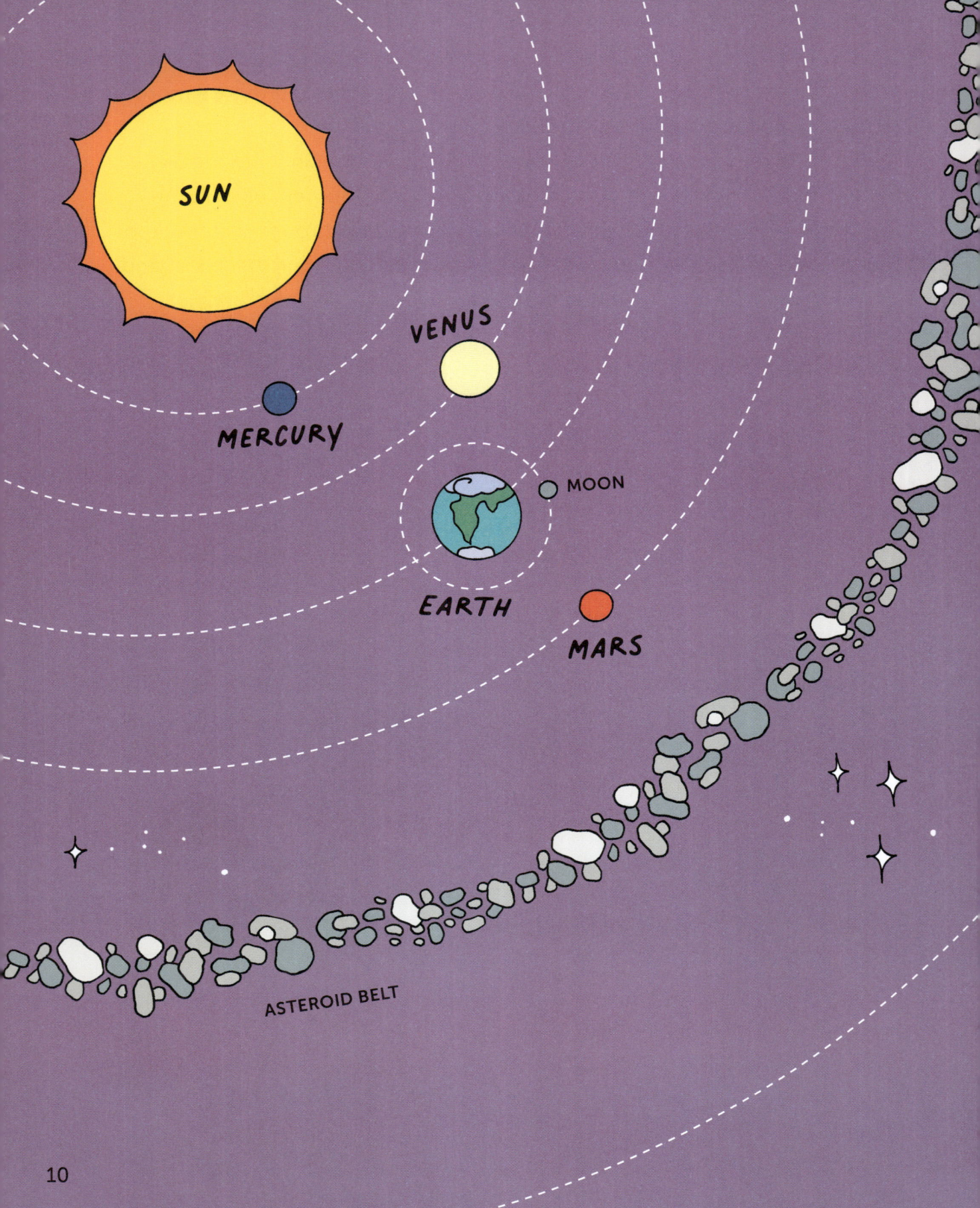

The Universe 14

The Big Bang 16

Atmosphere 18

Gravity 20

Speed of Light 22

The Solar System 24

Orbits 26

The Sun 28

The Moon 30

Moon Phases 32

Solar and
Lunar Eclipses 34

The Planets 36

Mercury 38

Venus 40

Earth 42

Mars 44

Jupiter 46

Saturn 48

Uranus 50

Neptune 52

Dwarf Planets 54

Pluto 56

Kuiper Belt 58

Asteroids and
the Asteroid Belt 60

The Big Picture

It's a big universe out there! Are you ready to explore the unknown? For hundreds of years, people thought that everything in space revolved around Earth. Now we know that's not true and our little planet is just one of *billions* of other planets. In fact, our home planet is only about 4.5 billion years old—less than half as old as the universe itself. In this section you'll learn all about the elements that make up the universe (even the things we can't see) and how the universe started (a *big* bang). This section is chock-full of fun facts about our little corner of the galaxy: the solar system! Have you ever wondered what a dwarf planet is? How much you would weigh on the moon? Or how fast light moves? This section covers all that and more. Turn the page and start exploring the universe!

The Universe

The universe is made up of everything we can see and everything we *can't* see. It sounds confusing but remember: everything that has existed or ever will exist is part of the universe—even time! About 80 percent of the universe is made up of things scientists can't measure but know are there (called dark matter and dark energy) because they affect things we *can* see, like stars and planets. The universe is about 13.8 billion years old.

FILL IN THE MISSING LETTERS.

1. U _ i _ _ rs _
2. Pl _ n _ _ s
3. D _ _ k M _ t _ _ r
4. _ a _ k _ ne _ g _
5. T _ m _

IN 1543, AN ASTRONOMER NAMED COPERNICUS REALIZED EARTH REVOLVED AROUND THE SUN, NOT THE OTHER WAY AROUND. COLOR COPERNICUS.

The Big Bang

Billions of years ago, the universe looked very different. It was a small, dense point called a singularity. That singularity exploded outward, and the building blocks of our world (tiny atoms that make up everything) started to form. Over billions of years, those atoms made the stars and galaxies we can see today. Scientists call this the big bang, and it's our best theory for how the universe formed. The universe is still moving away from the singularity point and gets a little bigger every day.

EACH GALAXY IS UNIQUE. CAN YOU FIND SIX PAIRS OF MATCHING GALAXIES?

CRACK THE CODE!

There's a name for scientists who study how the universe began and how it grows. Use the key to crack the code.

$\underline{\text{C}}\ \underline{\text{O}}\ \underline{\text{S}}\ \underline{\text{M}}\ \underline{\text{O}}\ \underline{\text{L}}\ \underline{\text{O}}\ \underline{\text{G}}\ \underline{\text{I}}\ \underline{\text{S}}\ \underline{\text{T}}\ \underline{\text{S}}$
 1   19   4   3   19   21   19   16   11   4   22   4

KEY

1	2	3	4	5	6	7	8	9	10	11	12	13
C	H	M	S	R	V	B	X	P	N	I	A	W

14	15	16	17	18	19	20	21	22	23	24	25	26
U	K	G	Z	E	O	Y	L	T	Q	F	J	D

Atmosphere

Surrounding our planet are layers of gases called the atmosphere. We call those gases air—it's what we breathe. The air is made up of mostly nitrogen gas—78 percent nitrogen, 21 percent oxygen, and about 1 percent argon gas. The closer you get to space, the less air is in each layer. In the highest layers of the atmosphere, there isn't enough air for a person to survive. If Earth were an apple, the atmosphere would be as thin as its skin.

TRACE THE NAMES OF THE LAYERS OF EARTH'S ATMOSPHERE.

TROPOSPHERE (0–10 miles above Earth)

STRATOSPHERE (10–31 miles above Earth)

OZONE LAYER (in the Stratosphere)

MESOSPHERE (31–53 miles above Earth)

THERMOSPHERE (53–375 miles above Earth)

EXOSPHERE (above 375 miles)

ASTRONAUTS FROM ALL OVER THE WORLD WORK TOGETHER ON A STATION THAT ORBITS EARTH IN THE THERMOSPHERE. CONNECT THE DOTS TO SEE THE INTERNATIONAL SPACE STATION!

Gravity

When you jump up in the air, you return to the ground because of gravity. An object's weight can change depending on the pull of gravity. On the moon, you would weigh one-sixth as much as you do on Earth because less gravity is pulling you down. Although weight can change, mass (the amount of substance in an object) stays the same. Objects with bigger mass (like a planet) have more gravity and a stronger pull on things around it.

FILL IN EACH BLANK WITH A WORD FROM THE WORD BANK.

1. Your _____ is the same no matter where you are.

2. You weigh _____ on the moon than you do on Earth.

3. Bigger planets have _____ gravity because they have more mass.

4. Your _____ changes in different places.

5. Things are heavy because _____ pulls them down.

| WEIGHT | GRAVITY | LESS |
| MASS | MORE | |

BIG ROCKETS HELP SPACESHIPS ESCAPE EARTH'S GRAVITY AND FLY INTO SPACE. CAN YOU SPOT SIX DIFFERENCES BETWEEN THESE ROCKET LAUNCHES?

Speed of Light

Light moves faster than anything else in the universe. In space, light travels at 186,292 miles per *second*! Because objects in space are so far away, we use light-years to describe their distance from us. A light-year is the distance light travels in one Earth year (about 6 *trillion* miles). Because the light takes so long to reach us, when you look up at stars and other objects in space, you're actually seeing them as they were in the past.

WHAT WOULD A SPACESHIP THAT COULD TRAVEL AT THE SPEED OF LIGHT LOOK LIKE? COLOR IT ANY WAY YOU WANT.

YOU CAN MAKE 339 WORDS OUT OF THE LETTERS IN LIGHT-YEAR, INCLUDING "EAR." CAN YOU COME UP WITH EIGHT MORE?

1. _____
2. _____
3. _____
4. _____
5. _____
6. _____
7. _____
8. _____

The Solar System

The solar system is our home in space. It's our sun (sol) and all the objects that orbit around it, including the eight planets, asteroids, moons, comets, and dwarf planets. The four planets closest to the sun—Mercury, Venus, Earth, and Mars—are called "terrestrial" planets because they're made up of rocks and metals and are solid. The Asteroid Belt separates them from the other four planets—gas giants Jupiter and Saturn and ice giants Uranus and Neptune. The solar system is about 4.6 billion years old.

FIND AND CIRCLE THE NAMES OF THE PLANETS IN OUR SOLAR SYSTEM.

MERCURY
VENUS
EARTH
MARS
JUPITER
SATURN
URANUS
NEPTUNE

```
S B H I N N C D G R V U X T V
M F N E R E H U E R S T O U T
K P X U I H P C L J N D U D B
T U T G S W M T I S O F J I E
V A D E P G M D U A R I P J C
S S F H T R A E D N V A D Q Y
Z R E R C T S M H T E S M Z B
L B T E A K V E H O P B V G Q
L N J T B Z E R P F S Y K V G
G Z D I V U A C T S Q Z E T V
I K J P F I N U B V H N I O L
D V R U Q J U R A N U S N G B
A M L J Z Q O Y A S V X N P W
M S E Y C B G I Q V K U L J Z
C B L D I G P O M H T O R B A
```

COLOR ALL THE COOL OBJECTS YOU CAN FIND IN OUR SOLAR SYSTEM.

Orbits

An orbit is when one object rotates around another object in space. Each orbit takes one year. Objects in orbit are called satellites. Earth's most famous satellite is the moon, which orbits around us while we orbit around the sun. Satellites can be natural like planets and moons or human-made like the International Space Station. Planetary orbits look round, but they're actually oval (also known as elliptical).

THERE ARE MORE THAN 7,000 HUMAN-MADE SATELLITES ORBITING EARTH. CAN YOU FIND SIX MATCHING PAIRS OF SATELLITES?

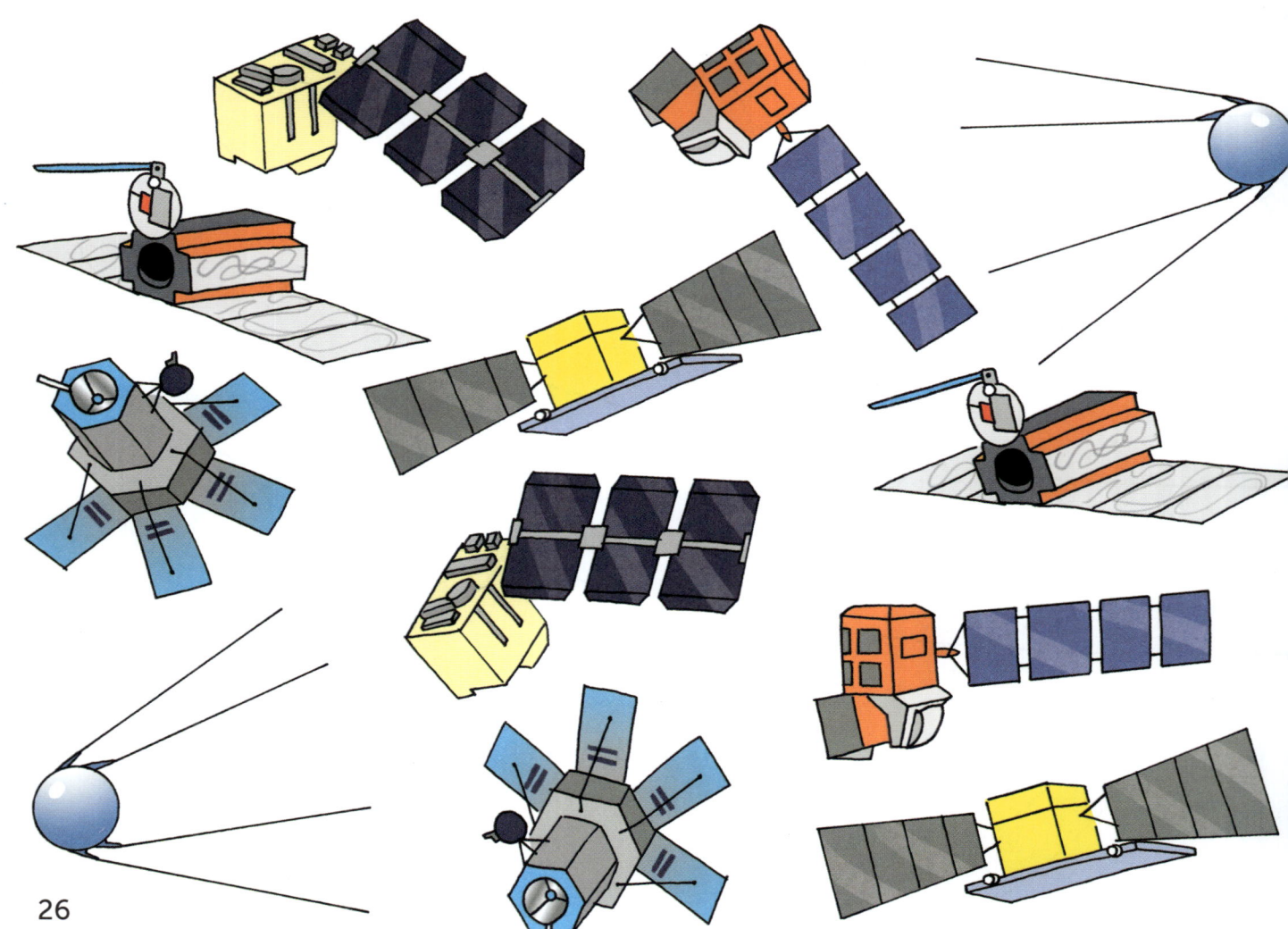

CAN YOU COMPLETE THIS CROSSWORD PUZZLE ABOUT ORBITS?

DOWN

1. Most orbits are this shape
2. Satellites can be _____ or human-made
5. The Earth orbits around the _____

ACROSS

3. An orbit is when something _____ around something else
4. Objects in orbit are called _____
6. Earth's most famous satellite

The Sun

The sun is the star at the center of our solar system. It's a huge, hot ball of plasma big enough to fit about 1.3 million Earths inside! At its core is a process called fusion that turns hydrogen into helium and gives off lots of heat and energy. This process is called nuclear fusion, and it makes life on Earth possible. The sun is an average-sized star. It is about 4.5 billion years old.

CRACK THE CODE!

Scientists have a word for when plants use sunlight to create energy. Use the key to crack the code.

__ __ __ __ __ -
10 26 7 16 7

__ __ __ __ __ __ __ __ __
6 17 12 16 26 1 6 4 6

KEY

1	2	3	4	5	6	7	8	9	10	11	12	13
E	D	L	I	Q	S	O	V	A	P	X	N	J

14	15	16	17	18	19	20	21	22	23	24	25	26
C	Z	T	Y	F	W	K	U	R	G	M	B	H

SOLAR FLARES—SUDDEN EXPLOSIONS OF ENERGY FROM THE SUN'S SURFACE—CAN CAUSE COLORFUL LIGHT SHOWS IN THE ATMOSPHERE. COLOR BY NUMBER TO SEE THE NORTHERN LIGHTS.

1. DARK BLUE
2. PURPLE
3. YELLOW-GREEN
4. GREEN
5. RED-VIOLET
6. YELLOW

The Moon

The moon is the brightest object in the night sky and Earth's only natural satellite. Its gravity causes the tides in the ocean. Scientists think it was formed after a planet-sized space object hit Earth billions of years ago. The moon looks close to us, but it's 230,000 miles away! When you look up at the moon, you can see all the craters from impacts of meteorites and asteroids. Because there's no wind on the moon, the craters stay there forever.

NEIL ARMSTRONG LANDED ON THE MOON IN 1969. COLOR THE MOON LANDING.

FIND AND CIRCLE THE LAST NAMES OF THE FIRST NINE ASTRONAUTS TO WALK ON THE MOON.

```
A P N G Z G H D M K H C U K O
I Y A P F Y R W A G E O S N G
R S E Q W A H R I N I R D L A
W C B M P J M I T C H E L L P
I L O E I S C S F E P D S H L
N E H G T L B L D R K V M E C
D S D R H M C V A C W N Z N G
F A O S Y V E W K U S L L U O
C N R O C T C G H S Z Q L L F
G S U N J O S T K M S C J I A
R N H B O Z T P Z N X P V E M
G S F E R C R T R S Z A C A N
I Q J J G V Y T K M A B H Q R C
S S U W M F N K R T H Q U R W
V E T V F U H P S W J D F N Y
```

ARMSTRONG   BEAN   SCOTT
ALDRIN   SHEPARD   IRWIN
CONRAD   MITCHELL   YOUNG

Moon Phases

The moon may look different every night, but it's not actually changing—it's a trick of the light. The moon doesn't shine; it reflects light from the sun. The moon seems to change depending on how much of it is in sunlight and how much is in darkness. These are called moon phases. During a full moon, the side of the moon that faces Earth is in light. At a new moon it's all in the dark. The other six phases are in between.

YOU CAN MAKE 360 WORDS OUT OF THE LETTERS IN MOON PHASES, INCLUDING "MOO." CAN YOU LIST EIGHT MORE?

1. _____
2. _____
3. _____
4. _____
5. _____
6. _____
7. _____
8. _____

TRACE THE LETTERS TO LEARN THE SIX PHASES OF THE MOON FROM NEW MOON TO FULL MOON AND BACK AGAIN!

WAXING CRESCENT

FIRST QUARTER

WAXING GIBBOUS

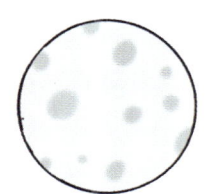

WANING GIBBOUS

THIRD QUARTER

WANING CRESCENT

Solar and Lunar Eclipses

An eclipse occurs whenever a planet or a moon gets in the way of the sun's light. It's like moving your hand over a flashlight to block the light. Eclipses happen on other planets, too. Here on Earth, we see both solar eclipses (where the moon blocks out the sun) and lunar eclipses (where Earth gets in the way of the moon reflecting sunlight and the moon goes dark). *Never* look straight at the sun during an eclipse (or any other time). It can burn your eyes!

ARE THESE FACTS TRUE OR FALSE? CIRCLE THE RIGHT ANSWER.

1. On Earth we have only one type of eclipse. TRUE FALSE

2. It's never safe to look straight at the sun. TRUE FALSE

3. Earth is the only planet with eclipses. TRUE FALSE

4. The sun blocks the moon during a solar eclipse. TRUE FALSE

5. The moon is dark during a lunar eclipse. TRUE FALSE

6. The sun's rays can hurt your eyes. TRUE FALSE

CAN YOU SPOT SIX DIFFERENCES BETWEEN THE SOLAR ECLIPSE (TOP) AND THE LUNAR ECLIPSE (BOTTOM)?

The Planets

Planets are large objects (like Earth) that orbit a star. A year is how long it takes the planet to orbit the star once. Planets also spin on themselves like a ball on a finger. That spin is one day. The length of days and years are different on every planet! In our solar system, we have three types of planets. The terrestrial planets (Mercury, Venus, Earth, and Mars) are closest to the sun. Gas giants (Jupiter and Saturn) and ice giants (Uranus and Neptune) have no solid ground. The word "planets" comes from the ancient Greek word for "wanderer."

IF YOU WATCHED THE SUN SET FROM MARS, IT WOULD LOOK BLUE. COLOR THE MARTIAN SUNSET.

UNSCRAMBLE THE NAMES OF THE PLANETS IN OUR SOLAR SYSTEM.

1. ECURMYR _____

2. UNSEV _____

3. TAERH _____

4. SRMA _____

5. TJPIREU _____

6. RSAUNT _____

7. NRAUUS _____

8. ENUNETP _____

Mercury

Mercury is the smallest planet in our solar system and the closest to the sun. On Mercury, the sun is 11 times brighter and looks three times bigger than on Earth. Mercury orbits the sun in just 88 days, which means that Mercury's year is only 88 days long. Mercury orbits the sun fast but spins slowly, so its days are very long—longer than its year! Because of its slow spin and fast orbit, Mercury has a sunrise only every 180 Earth days. It has no moon.

MATCH THE CLUES ON THE LEFT SIDE WITH THE CORRECT ANSWERS ON THE RIGHT SIDE.

1. Compared to other planets, Mercury is this size
2. Amount of days in a year on Mercury
3. Mercury's relation to the sun
4. The sun rises on Mercury after this many days
5. The sun looks this many times brighter from Mercury

A. 88
B. 11
C. 180
D. closest
E. smallest

A PROBE NAMED MESSENGER STUDIED MERCURY FROM SPACE. CONNECT THE DOTS TO SEE THE PROBE.

Venus

Even though Mercury is closest to the sun, Venus is the hottest planet in our solar system thanks to a thick atmosphere that traps heat. Venus spins in the opposite direction from most other planets, including Earth. Venus spins so slowly that one Venus day takes longer than a Venus year. Venus is Earth's closest planetary neighbor and can be seen in the night sky without a telescope. It has no moon.

COLOR THE VENERA PROBE PARACHUTING TO THE SURFACE OF VENUS.

40

CAN YOU COMPLETE THIS CROSSWORD PUZZLE ABOUT VENUS?

DOWN

2. You can see Venus on Earth without using this

3. On Venus a _____ is longer than a year

5. Venus doesn't have one of these

ACROSS

1. Venus is the _____ planet in our social system

4. Venus is so hot because of its thick _____

6. Venus spins in the _____ direction of most other planets

Earth

Earth—our home—is unique in lots of ways. It's the only planet we know of that supports life, the only planet with one moon, and the only planet with liquid water on the surface. Our atmosphere is made up of mostly nitrogen and has lots of oxygen for us to breathe. Day and night happen because of how Earth spins on itself, and seasons are caused by the tilt of Earth as we orbit the sun.

FILL IN EACH BLANK WITH A WORD FROM THE WORD BANK.

1. Earth is the only planet with _____ on its surface.

2. Our planet has only one _____.

3. Earth's _____ is full of nitrogen and oxygen.

4. The _____ are due to the angle of Earth.

5. Earth is the only planet we are sure supports _____.

MOON   SEASONS   ATMOSPHERE

LIFE   LIQUID WATER

EARTH IS OUR HOME! LEARN TO DRAW EARTH AND OUR MOON.

Mars

Mars is the fourth planet from the sun and the second-smallest planet in our solar system. It's called the "red planet" because of rusty iron on its surface. It's a cold planet with volcanoes, canyons, and polar ice caps made of frozen water. A Mars day is about 40 minutes longer than an Earth day. Because Mars is farther away from the sun and its orbit is bigger, a Mars year takes 687 Earth days. Mars has two potato-shaped moons: Phobos and Deimos.

CRACK THE CODE!

The largest volcano in the solar system is on Mars. Crack the code to learn its name.

___ ___ ___ ___ ___ ___ ___   ___ ___ ___ ___
 7   18   16   10   24   2   13   10   7   4   13

KEY

1	2	3	4	5	6	7	8	9	10	11	12	13
C	U	J	N	W	B	O	E	I	M	H	Z	S

14	15	16	17	18	19	20	21	22	23	24	25	26
X	G	Y	T	L	V	Q	A	R	F	P	K	D

CAN YOU SPOT SIX DIFFERENCES IN THESE TWO PICTURES OF THE MARS ROVER PERSEVERANCE?

Jupiter

Jupiter is the biggest planet in the solar system. If Earth were the size of a nickel, Jupiter would be a basketball. It doesn't have a solid surface. Instead, it is covered in swirling clouds of ammonia and water floating in hydrogen and helium. These clouds move around in stripes and change how the planet looks. The Great Red Spot is a storm that's raged for hundreds of years in Jupiter's atmosphere!

FIND AND CIRCLE THE NAMES OF PROBES THAT SEND US PICTURES OF JUPITER AND ITS MOONS.

- ULYSSES
- CASSINI
- PIONEER
- VOYAGER
- JUNO
- NEW HORIZONS
- GALILEO
- JUICE

```
R P F C A S S I N I J G V M U
O B I I P E G M W U Q O C W P
P E Z O S K C V N F T K E I G
Y L L S N M G O H U C W B D V
I B Y I M E B N E S E Y D L O
P L I C L R E P A O N U K G Y
U P C Y D A C R K M B H U V A
C A H F P S G E G V T S G B G
Q F C G V I B S M A A J L R E
P M U I R G R N A D A E F S R
R D G P A Z U M I A P C Q H B
A M L C Z J Z L G L Y I F P H
H F S J P M D L E B Z U R G P
S N O Z I R O H W E N J D B J
C J O L P G N H M O X S T Q L
```

JUPITER HAS MORE THAN 90 MOONS. HOW MANY MOONS CAN YOU FIND IN THIS PICTURE?

Saturn

Saturn is the second-largest planet in our solar system. It is famous for the rings of dust-covered ice and rock that surround it. Saturn isn't the only planet to have rings, but its rings—which extend 175,000 miles away from the planet—are the most dramatic in the solar system. Saturn is a gas giant that is mostly made up of hydrogen and helium. Saturn has more than 140 moons! The largest moon, Titan, is bigger than Mercury.

ARE THESE SATURN FACTS TRUE OR FALSE?

1. Saturn is the only planet in the solar system with rings. TRUE FALSE

2. It has a moon that's bigger than Mercury. TRUE FALSE

3. Saturn has the fewest moons of any planet. TRUE FALSE

4. It's a kind of planet known as a gas giant. TRUE FALSE

5. Saturn is the largest planet in the solar system. TRUE FALSE

6. The planet's atmosphere is made up hydrogen and helium. TRUE FALSE

Uranus

Uranus, the third-biggest planet in the solar system, is a cold and windy ice giant surrounded by 13 hard-to-see rings and 27 moons. It has a thick atmosphere of methane, hydrogen, and helium. The methane is what makes Uranus look blue! Uranus is the only planet to rotate on its side—like a ball rolling down a hill. One year on Uranus is the same as 87 Earth years.

URANUS WAS THE FIRST PLANET DISCOVERED WITH A TELESCOPE. CAN YOU FIND SIX MATCHING PAIRS OF TELESCOPES?

FILL IN THE MISSING LETTERS.

1. R __ n __ s
2. __ __ an __ s
3. M __ th __ n __
4. He __ i __ m
5. __ ydr __ g __ n
6. I __ e   __ ia __ t

Neptune

Neptune, an ice giant, is the farthest-away planet in our solar system. Neptune has lots of storms: one was as big as Earth! The planet is cold and windy, with gusts reaching 1,200 miles per hour. Neptune has five faint rings and 14 moons. The largest moon, Triton, was discovered just 17 days after the planet itself. Neptune has completed only one orbit since it was discovered in 1846.

FILL IN EACH BLANK WITH A WORD FROM THE WORD BANK.

1. Neptune was discovered in _____.

2. It's the _____ planet in our solar system.

3. Neptune has _____ hard-to-see rings.

4. Weather on Neptune is cold and _____.

5. _____ is Neptune's largest moon.

6. Neptune has _____ moons.

14	FIVE	TRITON
WINDY	1846	FARTHEST

VOYAGER 2 IS THE ONLY SPACECRAFT TO VISIT NEPTUNE. USE THE KEY BELOW TO COLOR BOTH.

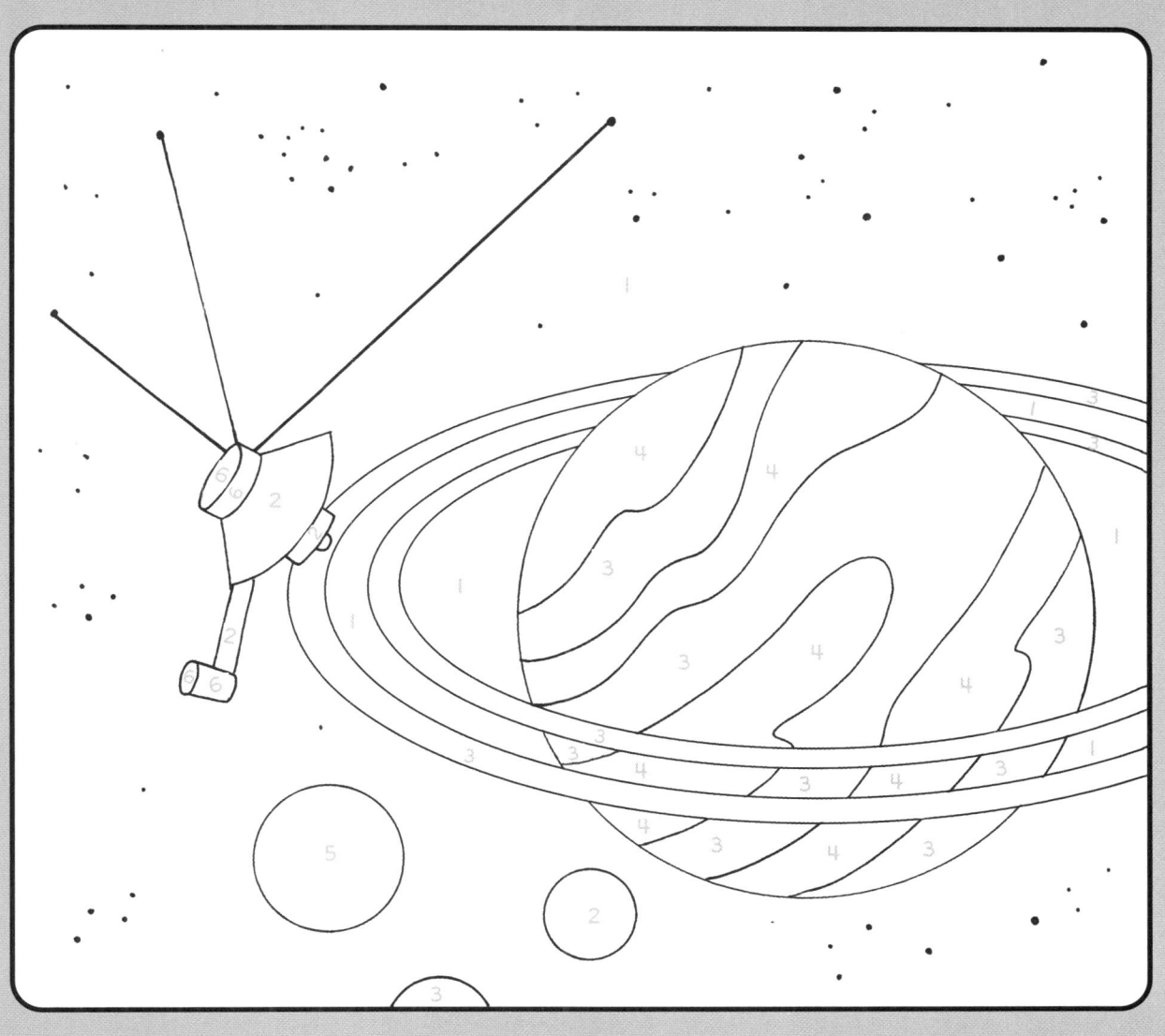

1. DARK BLUE
2. GRAY
3. BLUE
4. BLUE-GREEN
5. RED
6. BLACK

Dwarf Planets

The name "dwarf planet" has existed only since 2006. The International Astronomical Union, a worldwide organization of astronomers, defined dwarf planets as objects that orbit a star and are mostly round, but aren't big and heavy enough for their gravitational pull to clear their orbits of debris like a regular planet would. There are only five officially recognized dwarf planets—Pluto, Ceres, Makemake, Haumea, and Eris—but scientists think there are many more waiting to be discovered.

CAN YOU MATCH THE FIVE PAIRS OF DWARF PLANETS?

YOU CAN MAKE MORE THAN 1,000 WORDS OUT OF THE LETTERS IN DWARF PLANETS, INCLUDING "NET." CAN YOU LIST EIGHT MORE?

1. _____

2. _____

3. _____

4. _____

5. _____

6. _____

7. _____

8. _____

Pluto

Pluto is the most famous dwarf planet. It was our solar system's ninth planet for more than 70 years before it was demoted by the International Astronomical Union. Pluto is made of rock and ice and is full of mountains, valleys, craters, and glaciers. It's the largest object in the region beyond Neptune (known as the Kuiper Belt). Pluto's biggest moon, Charon, is nearly half the size of the planet. Pluto was named after the Roman god of the underworld by an 11-year-old girl!

UNSCRAMBLE THESE PLUTO WORDS.

1. RWAFD ETLAPN _____

2. RIGALCES _____

3. TOLUP _____

4. PUKIRE LEBT _____

5. NNTHI TAENPL _____

6. DEOUWLRRDN _____

A SPACE PROBE TOOK PHOTOS OF A GLACIER ON PLUTO'S SURFACE. CONNECT THE DOTS TO SEE THE SHAPE!

Kuiper Belt

The Kuiper Belt is an area of the solar system beyond Neptune's orbit. It's a doughnut-shaped region of space full of icy planetlike objects and comets. Pluto is the largest object in the Kuiper Belt. Scientists think the objects in the Kuiper Belt may be left over from the formation of the solar system. Compared to objects in the Asteroid Belt, Kuiper Belt objects tend to be bigger and icier. Scientists believe more than 70,000 of these objects exist.

NASA'S NEW HORIZONS SPACE PROBE IS THE ONLY SPACECRAFT THAT HAS VISITED THE KUIPER BELT. COLOR IT AS IT FLIES BY PLUTO.

CRACK THE CODE!

This small Kuiper Belt object is the most distant object ever explored by a spacecraft. Crack the code to learn its name.

__ __ __ __ __ __ __ __
22　1　1　3　8　3　7　17

KEY

1	2	3	4	5	6	7	8	9	10	11	12	13
R	I	O	M	G	V	T	K	B	Q	Y	D	W

14	15	16	17	18	19	20	21	22	23	24	25	26
Z	X	N	H	C	U	F	S	A	P	L	J	E

59

Asteroids and the Asteroid Belt

Asteroids are small, rocky objects that orbit the sun. They're smaller and more weirdly shaped than planets and are left over from the formation of our solar system. They're made of rock, clay, and metals like nickel and iron. Every asteroid is unique! Some are as small as pebbles while others are hundreds of miles wide. Between Mars and Jupiter is a region known as the Asteroid Belt where most of the asteroids live. The dwarf planet Ceres is also an asteroid in the Asteroid Belt.

SCIENTISTS HAVE COUNTED MORE THAN A MILLION ASTEROIDS. TRACE THE NAMES OF SOME OF THE BIGGEST.

CERES

VESTA

PALLAS

HYGIEA

INTERAMNIA

EUROPA

ABOUT 66 MILLION YEARS AGO, A GIGANTIC ASTEROID COLLIDED WITH EARTH AND WIPED OUT THE DINOSAURS. HOW MANY DINOSAURS CAN YOU FIND?

Stars 64

Constellations 66

Nebulas 68

Star Clusters 70

Life of a Star 72

Supernovas 74

Black Holes 76

Galaxies 78

The Milky Way 80

Comets 82

Meteoroids, Meteors, and Meteorites 84

The Show in the Sky

Look up in the night sky and try to count the stars. You can't! Astronomers think there could be up to one *septillion* stars in the universe (that's a 1 with 24 zeros after it). In our galaxy alone, scientists think there are 100 billion stars (a 1 with 11 zeros after it). In this section, you'll learn all about the different kinds of stars, the nebulas where stars are born, and what happens when stars die. Scientists can see all sorts of amazing things like stars with space probes and telescopes, but you can also see some very cool things on a dark night with just your own two eyes. Have you ever wished on a shooting star? It wasn't actually a star at all—it was a meteor burning up in the Earth's atmosphere! From constellations to comets and supernovas to star clusters, there's a lot to see in space. Get out your telescope: it's time to look up at the big show in the sky.

Stars

Stars are giant, glowing balls of hot plasma. Our sun is an averaged-sized star called a yellow dwarf. The biggest stars are called hypergiants. Stars are categorized in lots of ways, including color: blue stars are hotter than yellow stars, and yellow stars are hotter than red stars. Sirius—the brightest star in the night sky—is blueish white. When the sun gets old it will cool down and expand into a red giant star. (Don't worry, that won't happen for billions of years!)

STARS COME IN LOTS OF SIZES AND COLORS. CAN YOU MATCH SIX DIFFERENT PAIRS OF STARS?

CAN YOU SOLVE THIS STARRY CROSSWORD?

DOWN

1. Red stars are _____ than yellow stars
2. When the sun gets old it will become one of these
4. Our sun is a _____ dwarf
5. The brightest star in the night sky

ACROSS

3. These are the biggest stars in the universe
6. Blue stars are _____ than yellow stars
7. Glowing balls of _____ are stars

Constellations

Constellations are groups of stars that look like shapes. Long ago, people gave those shapes names—like Pegasus and Orion—and told stories about them. Stars in the 88 constellations aren't actually next to each other in space, even though they look close to one another from Earth. Asterisms are also shapes you can see in the sky, but they are generally smaller than constellations and may be part of a constellation. The Big Dipper, for example, is an asterism in the Ursa Major constellation.

FIND AND CIRCLE THE NAMES OF THESE FAMOUS CONSTELLATIONS IN THE WORD SEARCH.

URSA MAJOR
CENTAURUS
CASSIOPEIA
ORION
CANIS MAJOR
GEMINI
PEGASUS
PERSEUS

```
G E M I N I F J Z R U P D S V
W I J I F L H S O R G E U C L
Q R B Y A Y C J S Z A R V B F
A S C N T M A A R Z I S J V O
R L C K H M M K G I D E Y S N
B M A T S A A H Z C P U O J P
F I U I J A R M A C O S K T X
I A N O E E S P K T P E I K B
H A R Z R P Y M E P W O J K R
C N F B S A O N P G W D N V Q
L O H L C H P I B W A I N S H
F I A S E Z K O S M U S J C M
Y R G L Y T W C J S L K U P Y
J O K N E L H C M Z A D K S V
P G D S U R U A T N E C X A F
```

ONE OF THE EASIEST CONSTELLATIONS TO SEE IS THE HUNTER ORION. HIS BELT IS THREE BRIGHT STARS IN A ROW. CONNECT THE DOTS TO SEE ORION.

Nebulas

Nebulas are giant clouds of dust and gas (mostly hydrogen and helium) in the space between stars, which is called interstellar space. Most nebulas are bigger than our whole solar system! Some nebulas are formed from the explosion of dying stars. Other nebulas are areas of thick gases where stars are born. That's why nebulas are sometimes called "nurseries for new stars." The closest nebula to Earth is called the Helix Nebula; it's all that's left of a dying star.

TRACE THE NAMES OF THESE FAMOUS NEBULAS.

CAT'S EYE

HORSEHEAD

CARINA

OMEGA

TRIFID

LAGOON

Star Clusters

Star clusters are groups of stars, all about the same age, formed in the same cloud of gas. Clusters range from dozens of stars to millions of stars! Open star clusters are loose groups of a few hundred young stars. Globular clusters are groups of hundreds of thousands of stars packed close together. Pleiades, one of the brightest and closest star clusters, has more than 1,000 stars and is known as the Seven Sisters. You can easily spot its seven brightest stars from Earth.

MATCH THE CLUES ON THE LEFT SIDE WITH THE CORRECT ANSWERS ON THE RIGHT SIDE.

1. Another name for Pleiades
2. Small clusters of young stars
3. Clusters full of lots of stars
4. Where star clusters are formed
5. Number of stars in the Seven Sisters

A. more than 1,000
B. open star cluster
C. Seven Sisters
D. cloud of gas
E. globular clusters

THE SOUL NEBULA IS A STAR CLUSTER SURROUNDED BY A CLOUD OF DUST AND GAS. USE THE KEY BELOW TO COLOR THE SOUL NEBULA.

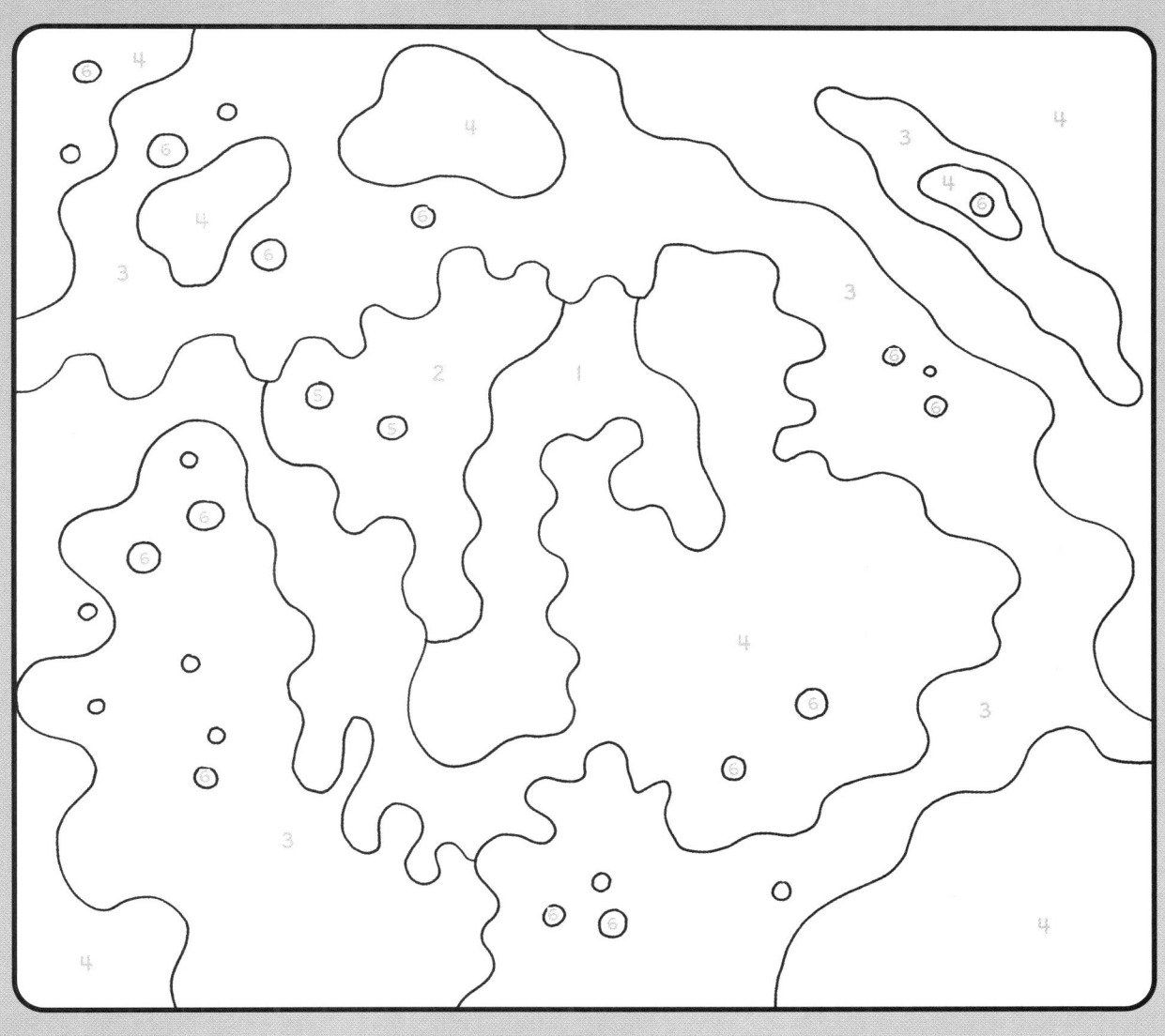

1. RED
2. ORANGE
3. GREEN
4. BLACK
5. YELLOW
6. BLUE

Life of a Star

Stars are born in large clouds of gas called nebulas and live for billions of years. They spend most of their lives turning hydrogen into helium to make heat and light. When they run out of hydrogen, they start to die. Average-sized stars, like the sun, use up their energy until they explode outward into red giants, shrink into white dwarfs, and fade into black dwarfs. Some big, heavy stars explode as supernovas and turn into black holes.

UNSCRAMBLE THESE STAR WORDS.

1. CLKAB OLEHS _____

2. LBENUSA _____

3. DRE NAGIST _____

4. TWIEH WRAFSD _____

5. EOHYGNRD _____

6. ASSRT _____

WHEN A STAR GOES SUPERNOVA IT DESTROYS THE PLANETS ORBITING IT! COLOR THIS EXPLODING STAR SYSTEM.

Supernovas

When the biggest and heaviest stars in our universe die, they explode into supernovas. A supernova explosion lasts only about 100 seconds, but light from the explosion can last for months. Some supernovas are so bright, they outshine the other stars in the galaxy and can even be seen on Earth during the day. Without supernovas there would be no life on Earth: all the elements in the sun, Earth, and even you are made of the stardust from supernova explosions pushing out into the rest of the universe!

LONG AGO, CHINESE ASTRONOMERS SAW A "GUEST STAR" (A SUPERNOVA) THAT APPEARED SUDDENLY IN THE SKY AND DISAPPEARED 8 MONTHS LATER. CAN YOU MATCH FIVE OF THEIR TOOLS?

YOU CAN MAKE 500 WORDS FROM THE LETTERS IN SUPERNOVAS, INCLUDING "SUN." CAN YOU FIND EIGHT MORE?

1. _____
2. _____
3. _____
4. _____
5. _____
6. _____
7. _____
8. _____

Black Holes

Black holes are areas in our universe that have a pull so strong that nothing, not even light, can escape. A black hole forms when a giant star dies. After it explodes in a supernova, it collapses back on a point no bigger than the tip of a pencil. Picture a black hole as a circle with a dot in the middle. The dot pulls everything in the circle inside it. Scientists think there are supermassive black holes at the center of almost every galaxy.

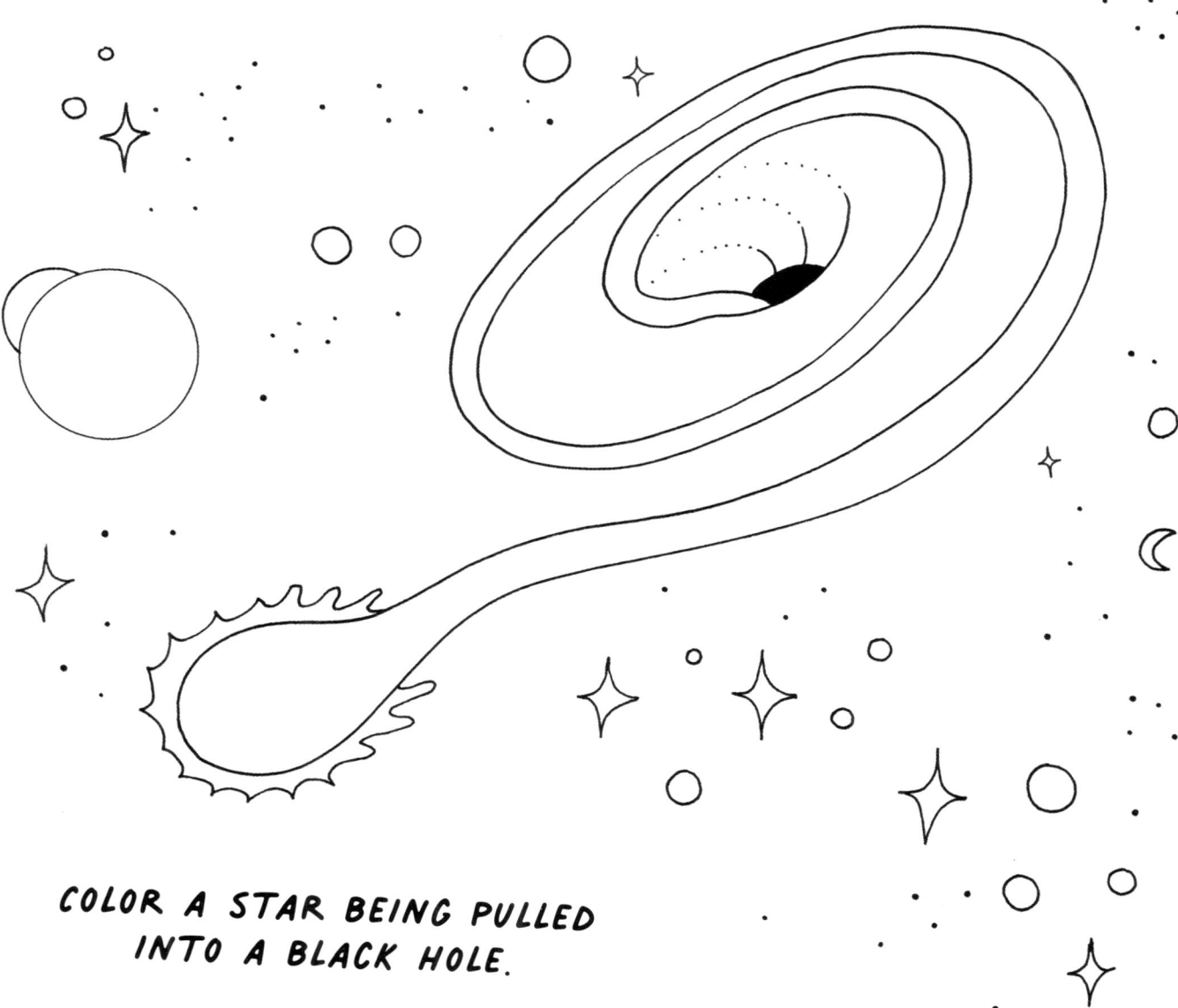

COLOR A STAR BEING PULLED INTO A BLACK HOLE.

CRACK THE CODE!

If you flew a spaceship into a black hole, the strong gravity would stretch the ship out into a long string. Crack the code to learn the word scientists use to describe this.

$\overline{20}\ \overline{24}\ \overline{22}\ \overline{2}\ \overline{8}\ \overline{26}\ \overline{9}\ \overline{9}\ \overline{15}$ -

$\overline{19}\ \overline{15}\ \overline{1}\ \overline{22}\ \overline{9}\ \overline{15}\ \overline{18}\ \overline{7}$

KEY

1	2	3	4	5	6	7	8	9	10	11	12	13
C	G	K	D	J	Q	N	H	T	R	W	Y	B

14	15	16	17	18	19	20	21	22	23	24	25	26
Z	I	V	U	O	F	S	L	A	X	P	M	E

Galaxies

A galaxy is a group of billions of stars and their planets, with gas, dust, and dark matter all held together by gravity. There are so many galaxies that we can't count them all. The Hubble telescope looked at a small patch of space for 12 days and found 10,000 galaxies! Scientists think there are more than 100 billion galaxies in the universe. There are three main galaxy shapes: spiral (like the Milky Way), elliptical (which are egg-shaped), and irregular (which don't fit either category).

CAN YOU SOLVE THIS GALACTIC CROSSWORD?

DOWN

1. A famous telescope that took pictures of galaxies

3. The Milky Way is this kind of galaxy

4. Galaxies are held together by this

ACROSS

2. There are more than 100 billion of these in the universe

5. Galaxies are made up of stars, planets, gas, dust, and this

6. These galaxies are egg-shaped

The Milky Way

The Milky Way galaxy is our home in the universe. Scientists think there are about 400 billion stars in our galaxy. That explains its name—there are so many stars that it looks like a milky-white band across the night sky. The Milky Way is so big it would take about 200,000 years for a spaceship traveling at the speed of light to cross it! Like many galaxies, it's held together by the gravity of a supermassive black hole in the center.

ON A DARK NIGHT, YOU CAN SEE THE PURPLES, ORANGES, AND DARK GREENS OF THE MILKY WAY. COLOR THIS NIGHT-TIME SCENE.

FIND AND CIRCLE THE NAMES OF SOME OF THE STARS IN THE MILKY WAY.

```
B S O C D J S R A E C B N G W
E A M R P K U I Y C S E Z W T
C R T C A H R G M P J T P N J
U C U Y B S U E C A P E L L A
O I T S I A T L M G V L F S N
E V T R H P C S Z L T G D O C
J G I E A L R V T C J E Z L T
N U J G C M A O S T C U G K R
S D E W B U A O C B F S P R A
J V I N G Y A L H Y A E M Y S
K W Z K Y C R T G K O T C A F
L O S I B T K E L M A N H R D
A Z N I S R G F H A C R F N E
Q J K S D M L A T P J E A V C
M L A B G Z P H J L S A H T G
```

BETELGEUSE   TAU CETI   CAPELLA

SIRIUS   ARCTURUS   PROCYON

SOL   VEGA   RIGEL

Comets

Comets are big balls of dust and ice that stream across space. At the center of a comet is a frozen rock of dust, ice, and gases called the nucleus. As comets move, dust and gas trail behind the nucleus, making most comets look like they have two long tails! In our solar system, comets come from the Kuiper Belt and the Oort cloud beyond it. Comets are left over from the formation of the solar system 4.6 billion years ago.

FILL IN EACH BLANK WITH A WORD FROM THE WORD BANK.

1. The center of a comet is called the _____.

2. Comets come from the _____ and the Oort Cloud.

3. Comets are _____ billion years old.

4. It looks like comets have _____ tails.

5. The center of a comet is _____.

6. Comets are big balls of dust and _____.

| KUIPER BELT | ICE | 4.6 |
| TWO | FROZEN | NUCLEUS |

CAN YOU SPOT SIX DIFFERENCES IN THESE PICTURES OF KIDS WATCHING HALLEY'S COMET?

Meteoroids, Meteors, and Meteorites

When asteroids or comets collide, tiny pieces of rock break off into space. These are called meteoroids. When a meteoroid gets close enough to Earth to burn up in our atmosphere, it's called a meteor. Have you ever seen a shooting star? It was actually a meteor! Some meteor showers happen every year, where hundreds of meteors flash across the night sky in a short time. Meteors that make it through the atmosphere to crash into Earth are called meteorites.

FILL IN THE MISSING LETTERS.

1. _ ete _ _
2. S _ oo _ i _ _   _ t _ r
3. M _ te _ r _ ids
4. C _ me _ s
5. _ s _ _ ro _ d _
6. _ et _ o _ it _ s

Satellites 88

Rockets 90

Rovers 92

Space Probes 94

Spaceplanes 96

Space Explorers 98

Astronauts 100

Spacesuits 102

Living and
Working in Space 104

Moon Missions 106

Mars Missions 108

International
Space Station 110

Telescopes 112

Aliens 114

UFOs 116

Space Tourism 118

Our Place in Space

Since the invention of the telescope, people have dreamed of exploring the universe. For hundreds of years, we observed the stars from the ground, but in the mid-1900s everything changed. The "space race" between the United States and the Soviet Union led to satellites orbiting Earth, interstellar probes, space telescopes, and space stations. In less than 50 years, we went from the first man in space (1961) to the first steps on the moon (1969) to human beings living full-time on the International Space Station (2000 to now)! Thanks to technology, we learn more about our corner of the universe every day—and we learn more about what exists beyond our reach. Now scientists are planning to land humans on Mars! Would you want to be an astronaut orbiting Earth? What about living on another planet? Think about what people accomplished during the first 50 years of the space age and ask yourself: What can we do in the next 100 years? Dream big, turn the page, and blast off!

Satellites

A satellite is an object that orbits a larger object. The moon is Earth's only natural satellite. But for decades, scientists have been launching artificial satellites into orbit around our planet. Except for special space stations, no one lives on satellites. They're important to everyday life and help us with everything from weather forecasts to navigation to communications. Some satellites are used for countries to spy on each other, and others, like the Hubble telescope, take pictures of faraway things in space.

SOME SATELLITES ORBIT EARTH TO STUDY WEATHER PATTERNS. COLOR THE SATELLITE (AND SPOT THE STORM ON EARTH).

CRACK THE CODE!

In 1957, the Soviet Union launched the first artificial satellite into Earth's orbit. Crack the code to learn its name.

$\overline{}\ \overline{}\ \overline{}\ \overline{}\ \overline{}\ \overline{}\ \overline{}$
21 23 7 14 5 3 9

KEY

1	2	3	4	5	6	7	8	9	10	11	12	13
E	H	I	Q	N	B	U	Z	K	Y	D	X	R

14	15	16	17	18	19	20	21	22	23	24	25	26
T	O	M	J	F	A	W	S	V	P	L	G	C

Rockets

The word "rocket" describes a type of engine *and* the vehicle that uses a rocket engine to move. Rockets create thrust, a combination of fuel and air, that surges out of the back of the engine and pushes the spacecraft forward. Rockets are shaped like cylinders with pointed tops so they don't meet resistance in Earth's atmosphere; they're aerodynamic. To escape Earth's gravity, rockets move 4.9 miles *per second* (about 17,000 miles per hour). Rockets were first used in China long ago for fireworks and weapons.

UNSCRAMBLE THESE ROCKET-POWERED WORDS.

1. INEEGN
2. KRIFOSWER
3. HURSTT
4. CPAFTSECAR
5. KERTOSC
6. DMNAROEACIY

SOVIET COSMONAUT YURI GAGARIN WAS THE FIRST HUMAN TO FLY IN OUTER SPACE. HIS SPACESHIP, THE VOSTOK 1, WAS STRAPPED TO R-7 ROCKETS. LEARN TO DRAW HIS SHIP AS IT BLASTS OFF.

Rovers

Rovers are electric vehicles that help scientists explore and understand planets, moons, and other space objects by taking photos and analyzing soil and rock samples. While some rovers, like the moon buggy from the Apollo missions, are driven by astronauts, most are robots that are given instructions from Earth. The first human-made rover was the *Lunokhod 1* from the Soviet Union, which landed on the moon in 1970 and operated for nearly a year.

FIND AND CIRCLE THE NAMES OF THESE SPACE ROVERS.

- LUNOKHOD
- SOJOURNER
- OPPORTUNITY
- CURIOSITY
- PERSEVERANCE
- SPIRIT
- YUTU
- PRAGYAN
- ZHURONG

```
L Z V O H R B C D H S T M Y C
S U H E T L R S Y N G A F D L
A L N U C N S H R O J E C A P
M A L O R N V M I K L C R J X
S A B R K O A L G U Q O U L Q
O H Y A K H N R O A P S Q T R
J L R E D N O G E P E G F I Q
O V P B H Y A D O V Z S C R A
U Y T I S O I R U C E B G I G
R C K D Z W T V I I R S W P G
N H Z I A U B S Z L O Z R S C
E H Z U N P R A G Y A N W E U
R W T I G J A D S T V W B G P
A U T N D P W L A I L R Z S Y
Y Y L M K C A I B G N P V E L
```

OPPORTUNITY IS ONE OF SIX ROBOTIC ROVERS SENT TO THE SURFACE OF MARS. HELP "OPPY" FIND ITS NEXT ROCK TO SAMPLE!

Space Probes

Space probes are small, unmanned spacecraft that are used to explore far-away planets, moons, and asteroids. Sometimes probes stay in orbit around a planet or moon for years and use radio waves to send information back to Earth, but others are designed to fly by or even crash into objects. The probe Voyager is NASA's longest-lived mission. Launched in 1977, it's still operating today. The twin Voyager 1 and Voyager 2 probes are the only spacecraft to ever explore interstellar space!

PROBES SEND BACK INFORMATION FROM FAR AWAY FOR SCIENTISTS TO STUDY. COLOR THIS JUPITER PROBE.

TRACE THE NAMES OF THESE FAMOUS SPACE PROBES.

CASSINI

JUNO

PIONEER

HELIOS

MARINER

NEW HORIZONS

Spaceplanes

Until 1981, astronauts going into space used a brand-new capsule on top of a rocket and returned to Earth in the capsule, using a parachute. The NASA space shuttle was the world's first reusable spacecraft and the first spaceplane. Like traditional spaceships, spaceplanes orbit Earth and dock with the International Space Station, but they can also land on a runway like a regular airplane. Some spaceplanes, like the NASA shuttle, carry astronauts, while others carry only supplies and are operated from Earth.

ARE THESE SPACEPLANE FACTS TRUE OR FALSE? CIRCLE THE RIGHT ANSWER.

1. Spaceplanes were the first type of spacecraft.
   TRUE FALSE

2. Spaceplanes use a parachute during descent. TRUE FALSE

3. The first reusable spaceship was the space shuttle.
   TRUE FALSE

4. All spaceplanes carry people. TRUE FALSE

5. Spaceplanes land on runways like airplanes. TRUE FALSE

6. Spaceplanes can dock with the International Space Station.
   TRUE FALSE

CONNECT THE DOTS TO SEE THE MOST FAMOUS SPACEPLANE— THE NASA SPACE SHUTTLE.

97

Space Explorers

When the "space race" began, no one knew if living things could survive going into space. In 1957, Laika, a stray dog from Russia, became the first creature to orbit Earth. Since then, more than 600 astronauts from over 30 countries have traveled to space and worked on spaceships and space stations, taken space walks, and even walked on the moon. In the future, space explorers could make it to Mars and beyond—helping us learn more about our solar system and our place in the universe.

FILL IN THE MISSING LETTERS.

1. S__ac__ R__ce
2. E____lor__rs
3. __pa__e W__l__s
4. L__i__a
5. __st__o__a__ts

ASTRONAUTS GO ON SPACE WALKS TO DO EXPERIMENTS AND REPAIR EQUIPMENT. CAN YOU SPOT SIX DIFFERENCES BETWEEN THESE SPACEWALKS?

Astronauts

Astronauts are trained to travel, work, and even live in outer space. In Russia, they're called cosmonauts, and in China they're known as taikonauts. The first astronauts were jet pilots. Astronauts undergo hundreds of hours of training to prepare for missions. Early space missions were only a few hours long, but now astronauts spend an average of six months living in space before coming back to Earth! The word "astronaut" means "space sailor" in Greek.

TO HELP PREPARE FOR SPACE, ASTRONAUTS TRAIN UNDERWATER AT THE NEUTRAL BUOYANCY LABORATORY, WHICH HAS AN IMITATION INTERNATIONAL SPACE STATION IN A GIANT POOL. COLOR THE SCENE.

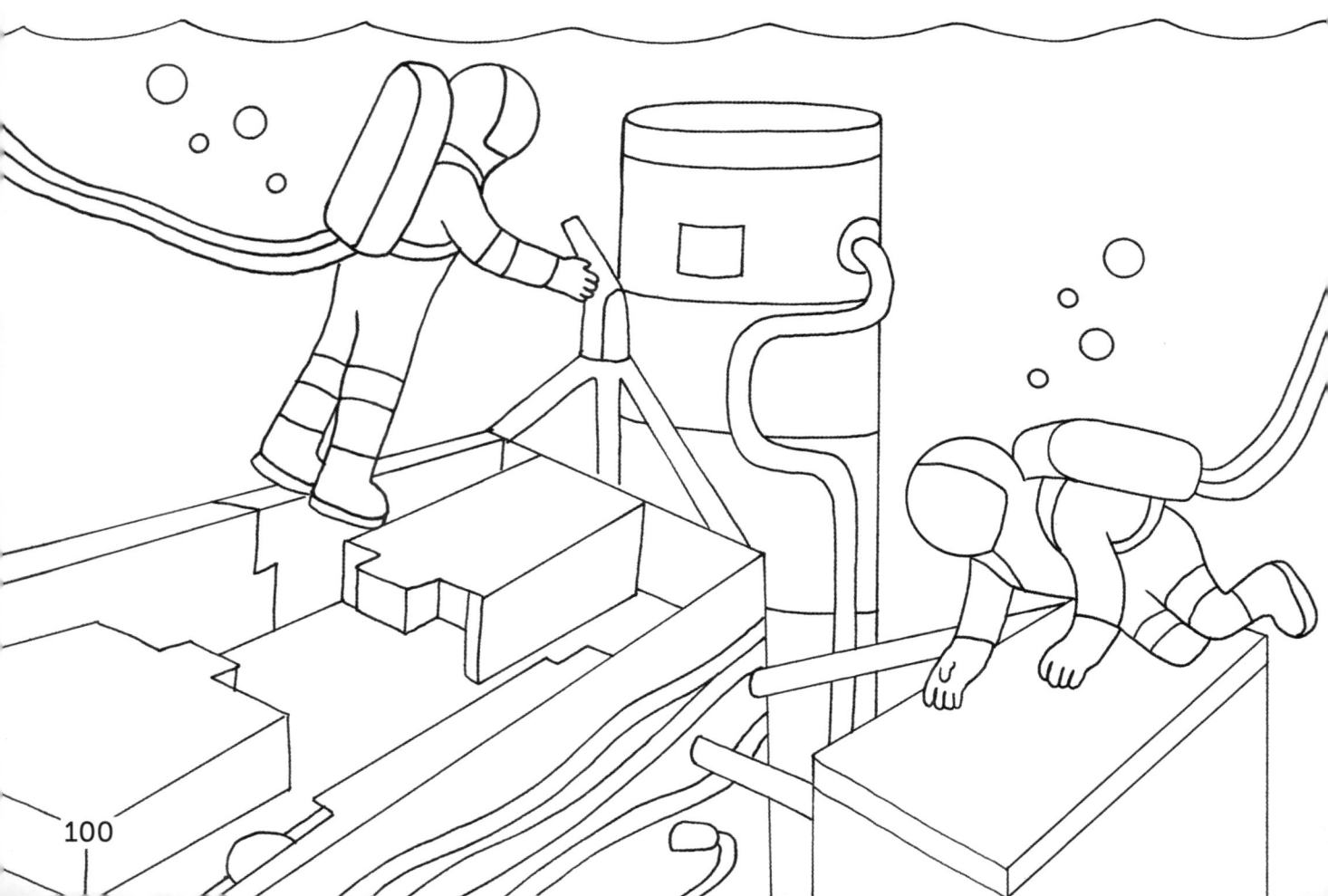

FIND AND CIRCLE THE NAMES OF THE FIRST NINE PEOPLE IN SPACE.

```
W I N H G B N Y M S F N I V C
P S J C Y N F I A O I L S O C
O G J C F Q N H K M S A D T M
P X P J E N K T M O O S H I E
V T M G E J R J V Y L G I T R
I O F L D R A P E H S A G R S
C T G Z C H S I F S J A Y C G
H R F M T V L R B C G B H E I
F U Y P N T F U P A Q I G F V
C A R P E N T E R U R F K K J
T P N I C M I I N R Y D S T M
Z Q L K I F N C A G M K W A S
L Q D H P L C I W D B D Z I Q
S E H N J Y F S R C S R T M P
A G J M K S Q Z V H Z O T P K
```

GAGARIN   TITOV   NIKOLAYEV
SHEPARD   GLENN   POPVICH
GRISSOM   CARPENTER   SCHIRRA

Spacesuits

In space, astronauts wear special suits that cover their entire bodies. They provide air to breathe and keep astronauts protected against extreme radiation and temperature. Spacesuits have big helmets with clear visors over the head and face, thick gloves, oxygen tanks, flexible arm and leg joints, boots, and radios for communication. If you tried to go into space without a spacesuit, you would die in under a minute. The lack of atmospheric pressure would make the blood in your body boil.

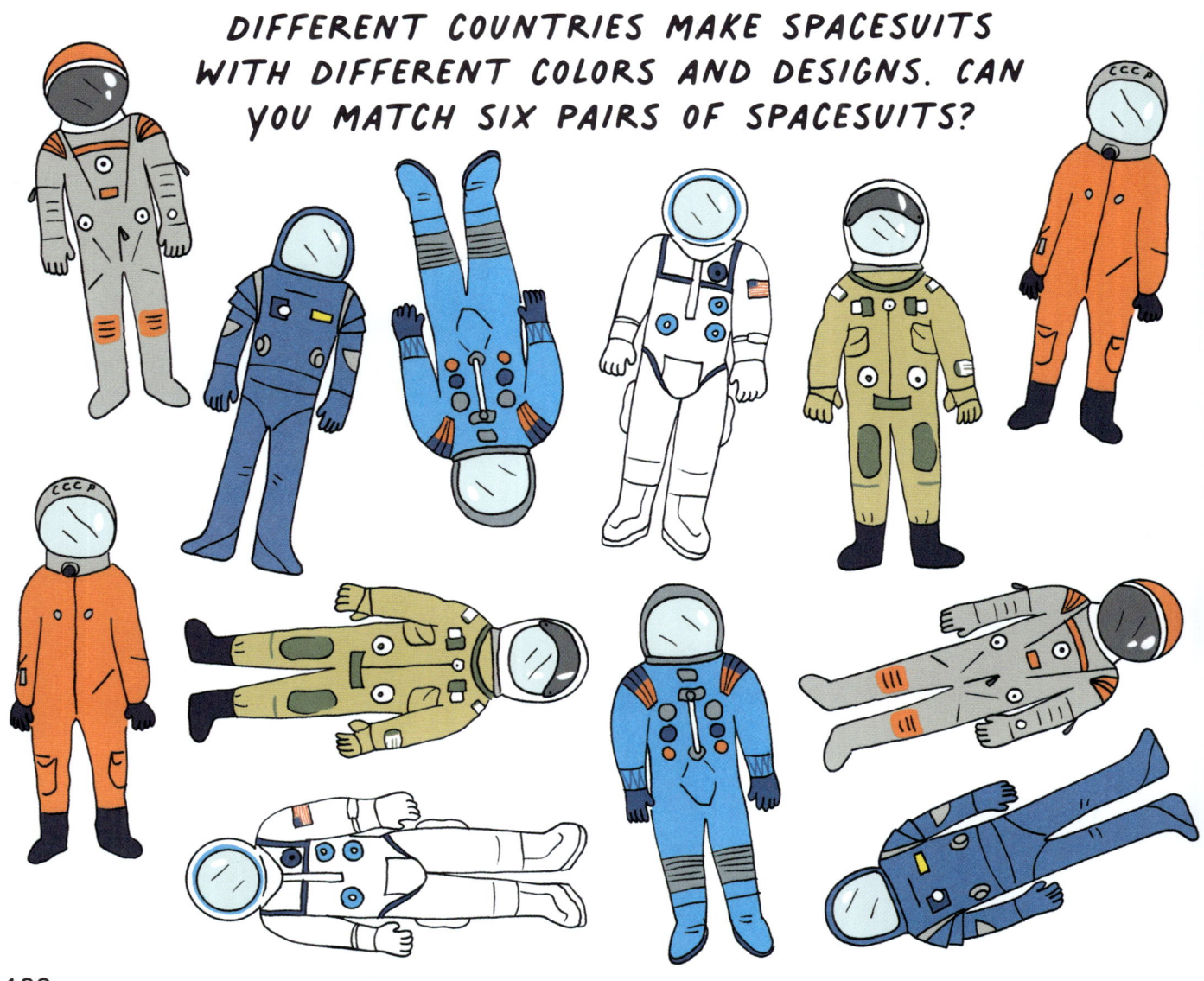

DIFFERENT COUNTRIES MAKE SPACESUITS WITH DIFFERENT COLORS AND DESIGNS. CAN YOU MATCH SIX PAIRS OF SPACESUITS?

YOU CAN MAKE MORE THAN 400 WORDS OUT OF THE LETTERS IN SPACESUITS, INCLUDING "ACE." CAN YOU LIST EIGHT MORE?

1. _____
2. _____
3. _____
4. _____
5. _____
6. _____
7. _____
8. _____

Living and Working in Space

In space, astronauts eat, work, exercise, and sleep. But they do it all in zero gravity! On space stations, astronauts strap themselves in to sleep and use grab bars to move around (and go to the bathroom). They can't shower since water doesn't flow down without gravity, so they take sponge baths. They perform science experiments, help with repairs, and communicate with scientists on Earth. They have to exercise at least two hours a day so they don't lose muscle or get weak bones from weightlessness.

ARE THESE FACTS TRUE OR FALSE? CIRCLE THE RIGHT ANSWER.

1. Astronauts can walk normally in space. TRUE FALSE

2. Exercise is extra important in space. TRUE FALSE

3. Astronauts can get weak if they are in space too long. TRUE FALSE

4. Sleeping in space is the same as on Earth. TRUE FALSE

5. Astronauts use grab bars to move around. TRUE FALSE

6. Astronauts take normal baths and showers on space stations. TRUE FALSE

ASTRONAUTS LIVE AND WORK ON THE INTERNATIONAL SPACE STATION. CAN YOU SPOT SIX DIFFERENCES BETWEEN THESE SPACE STATION SCENES?

Moon Missions

In 1961, President Kennedy challenged America to put astronauts on the moon within that decade, and in 1969, Apollo 11 landed on the moon with Neil Armstrong (the first man on the moon), Buzz Aldrin (the second man on the moon), and Michael Collins. Twelve American astronauts visited the moon from 1969 to 1972 (but no one since). The international Artemis program, led by NASA, will send astronauts back to the moon by 2030 and eventually build Lunar Gateway to orbit the moon—the first ever space station outside of Earth's orbit!

EVERY SPACE MISSION HAS A UNIQUE PATCH. CAN YOU FIND SIX MATCHING PAIRS OF APOLLO MISSION PATCHES?

HOW MUCH DO YOU KNOW ABOUT MISSIONS TO THE MOON? COMPLETE THE CROSSWORD.

DOWN

1. First man to walk on the moon
3. The president who challenged NASA to go to the moon
4. The name of the space station planned to orbit the moon
6. The program that took the first astronauts to the moon

ACROSS

2. The program that will send astronauts back to the moon
5. Second man to walk on the moon

Mars Missions

Mars is the only planet in the solar system inhabited entirely by robots! Six rovers have landed on the "red planet"—five from the United States and one from China. In 1971, a Soviet Union probe became the first object from Earth to make it all the way to Mars. Because Mars is the planet most like Earth and has the most potential to support life as we know it, space agencies hope to send astronauts to Mars within the next 25 years.

PROBES AND ROVERS HAVE COLLECTED LOTS OF INFORMATION ABOUT ELEMENTS FOUND ON MARS. CAN YOU FIND AND CIRCLE THEM IN THIS WORD SEARCH?

SILICON

OXYGEN

IRON

MAGNESIUM

ALUMINUM

CALCIUM

POTASSIUM

TITANIUM

```
A F I G N O C M P J T N Q G D
E G T Y A X S O K T L E C R G
C S N B R L T P P M J G A N I
G D F L I A U S B C W Y L R Y
P L B W S K T M R O V X C L E
N I P S T K Z V I K C O I F C
M O I Y S R V C H N I E U D L
A U C M A G N E S I U M M L R
M R E I D C C Z S L K M B W S
Z Q M B L M N D N L V A I Q W
T G Z P U I K F N U A B J H O
Y G E V D K S O L B V P D L U
A Y I Y E S R H O B H G D W K
O M F M H I S E C H Z H P L H
J L T G M M U I N A T I T D K
```

USE THE KEY TO COLOR THE FUTURE FIRST ASTRONAUTS ON MARS!

1. ORANGE
2. RED
3. BLUE
4. GRAY
5. BLACK
6. BLUE-GREEN
7. GREEN

International Space Station

Astronauts from around the world work together on the International Space Station (ISS). The ISS is a space laboratory about the size of a football field where astronauts experiment with plants, bugs, robots, and more. It was too big to be built on Earth and sent into space, so it was constructed in space! Most astronauts live on the ISS for at least a few months. The ISS orbits Earth every 90 minutes, which means the crew sees 16 sunrises and sunsets every day!

COLOR THE ANIMALS SENT TO SPACE TO BE STUDIED ON THE ISS.

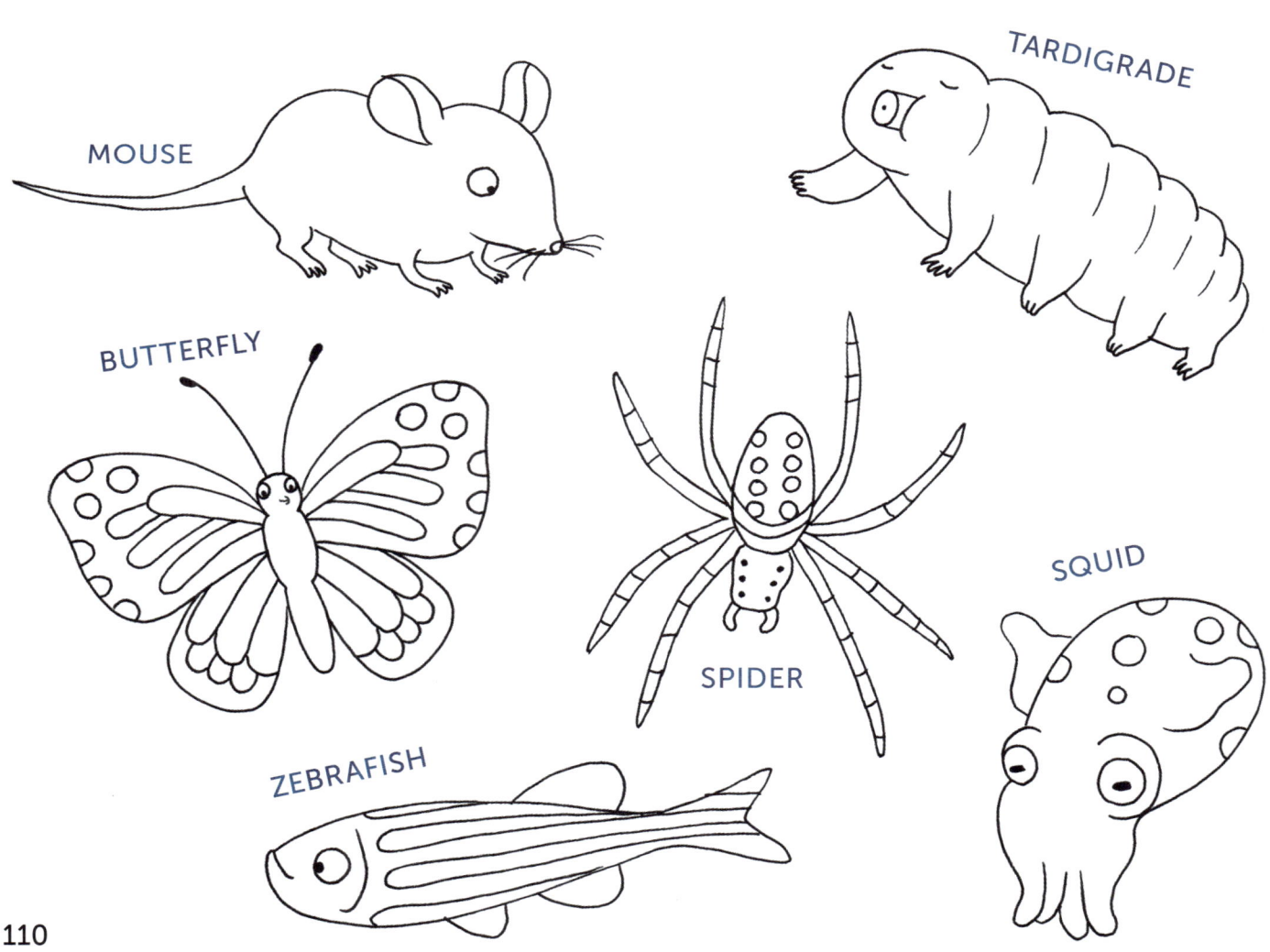

TRACE THE LETTERS TO LEARN THE NAMES OF SOME OF THE LARGEST SPACE AGENCIES IN THE WORLD.

NASA (UNITED STATES)
NATIONAL AERONAUTICS AND SPACE ADMINISTRATION

ROSCOSMOS (RUSSIA)
ROSCOSMOS STATE CORPORATION FOR SPACE ACTIVITIES

ESA (EUROPE)
EUROPEAN SPACE AGENCY

JAXA (JAPAN)
JAPAN AEROSPACE EXPLORATION AGENCY

ISRO (INDIA)
INDIAN SPACE RESEARCH ORGANIZATION

CNSA (CHINA)
CHINA NATIONAL SPACE ADMINISTRATION

Telescopes

People have used telescopes for hundreds of years to look into space. Observatories on Earth have huge telescopes that help scientists see distant objects like planets, comets, galaxies, and nebulas. To see even farther away, scientists place powerful space telescopes in orbit. The Hubble telescope launched in 1990 and helped us understand our place in the universe. The James Webb Space Telescope, which launched in 2021, is the largest, most powerful space telescope ever built.

FILL IN THE MISSING LETTERS.

1. __ __ le __ co __ e
2. __ rbi __
3. __ ist __ n __
4. O __ s __ rv __ t __ r __ __ s
5. H __ bb __ e
6. __ eb __ l __ s

THE TWIN TELESCOPES AT THE KECK OBSERVATORY IN HAWAII ARE SO POWERFUL THEY CAN SEE FARTHER INTO SPACE THAN THE HUBBLE TELESCOPE! CAN YOU SPOT SIX DIFFERENCES BETWEEN THESE TWO SCENES?

Aliens

Billions of planets like Earth exist, so it makes sense that life might have evolved on another planet like it did on Earth. It would probably be a place with liquid water and a breathable atmosphere. The SETI (Search for Extraterrestrial Intelligence) program scans for evidence of advanced alien civilizations in the universe. So far, no concrete proof of alien civilizations has been found. Lots of people picture little green men when they think of aliens, but alien life in our solar system will probably look more like tiny microbes or bacteria.

CAN YOU MATCH SIX PAIRS OF FICTIONAL ALIENS?

CRACK THE CODE!

There's a name for a scientist who studies the possibility of life beyond Earth. Crack the code to learn it!

$\overline{}_{5}\ \overline{}_{7}\ \overline{}_{20}\ \overline{}_{10}\ \overline{}_{18}\ -$

$\overline{}_{16}\ \overline{}_{12}\ \overline{}_{18}\ \overline{}_{8}\ \overline{}_{18}\ \overline{}_{1}\ \overline{}_{12}\ \overline{}_{7}\ \overline{}_{20}$

KEY

1	2	3	4	5	6	7	8	9	10	11	12	13
G	P	K	Z	A	W	S	L	N	R	C	I	Y

14	15	16	17	18	19	20	21	22	23	24	25	26
H	V	B	F	O	U	T	E	Q	X	M	J	D

UFOs

People talking about UFOs (unidentified flying objects) usually mean alien spacecraft, but most UFO sightings end up being test planes, spy craft, or weather balloons. In 1947, an unusual object crashed in the desert in Roswell, New Mexico, and was recovered by army officers. It was described as a "flying disk" or "flying saucer" and is considered the most famous UFO incident. The U.S. government investigates UFO sightings, but so far there has been no proof of alien activity in Earth's skies.

YOU CAN MAKE MORE THAN 2,000 WORDS OUT OF THE LETTERS IN UNIDENTIFIED FLYING OBJECT, INCLUDING "FLY." CAN YOU LIST EIGHT MORE?

1. _____
2. _____
3. _____
4. _____
5. _____
6. _____
7. _____
8. _____

Space Tourism

Visiting space for fun rather than science or exploration is called space tourism. From 2001 to 2009, seven space tourists visited the International Space Station using Russian Soyuz spacecraft. Each flight costs more than $20 million per person! Since then, a few companies let people travel into Earth's orbit, where they can experience a few minutes of weightlessness before coming back to Earth. People who pay to go into space aren't astronauts; they are "spaceflight participants" or "space tourists."

UNSCRAMBLE THESE SPACE TOURISM WORDS.

1. CPEAS UTTOSIR _____

2. CAPSAECFTR _____

3. EISESSSWELTHGN _____

4. IBTOR _____

5. NTPIPATRCAI _____

6. NUTSASROTA _____

MAYBE ONE DAY, YOUR GREAT-GREAT-GRANDCHILDREN WILL FLY TO THE MOON THE SAME WAY YOU FLY TO ANOTHER COUNTRY! COLOR THIS MOON TRAVEL POSTER.

Answer Key

Page 14
1. Universe
2. Planets
3. Dark Matter
4. Dark Energy
5. Time

Page 17
COSMOLOGISTS

Page 20
1. mass
2. less
3. more
4. weight
5. gravity

Page 21

Page 24

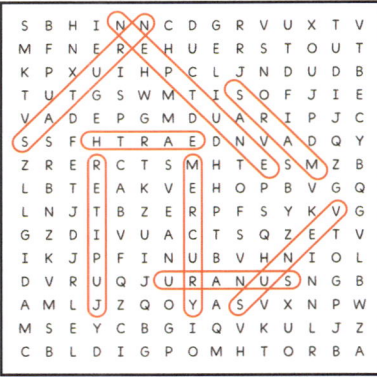

Page 27
1. ELLIPTICAL
2. NATURAL
3. ROTATES
4. SATELLITES
5. SUN
6. MOON

Page 28
PHOTOSYNTHESIS

Page 31

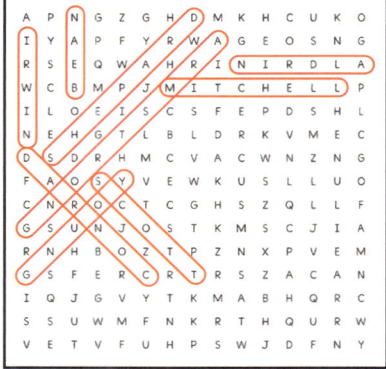

Page 34
1. False
2. True
3. False
4. False
5. True
6. True

Page 35

Page 37
1. MERCURY
2. VENUS
3. EARTH
4. MARS
5. JUPITER
6. SATURN
7. URANUS
8. NEPTUNE

Page 38
1. E
2. A
3. D
4. C
5. B

Page 41

1. HOTTEST
2. TELESCOPE
3. DAY
4. ATMOSPHERE
5. MOON
6. OPPOSITE

Page 42

1. liquid water
2. moon
3. atmosphere
4. seasons
5. life

Page 44

OLYMPUS MONS

Page 45

Page 46

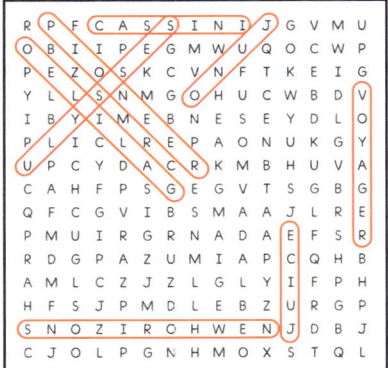

Page 47

19 moons

Page 48

1. False
2. True
3. False
4. True
5. False
6. True

Page 49

Page 51

1. Rings
2. Uranus
3. Methane
4. Helium
5. Hydrogen
6. Ice Giant

Page 52

1. 1846
2. farthest
3. five
4. windy
5. Triton
6. 14

Page 56

1. DWARF PLANET
2. GLACIERS
3. PLUTO
4. KUIPER BELT
5. NINTH PLANET
6. UNDERWORLD

Page 59

ARROKOTH

Page 61

11 dinosaurs

Page 65

1. COOLER
2. RED GIANT
3. HYPERGIANTS
4. YELLOW
5. SIRIUS
6. HOTTER
7. PLASMA

Page 66

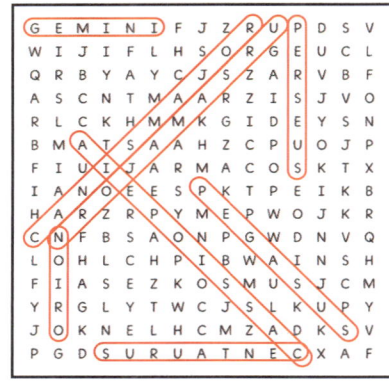

Page 69

45 stars

Page 70

1. C
2. B
3. E
4. D
5. A

Page 72

1. BLACK HOLES
2. NEBULAS
3. RED GIANTS
4. WHITE DWARFS
5. HYDROGEN
6. STARS

Page 77

SPAGHETTIFICATION

Page 78

1. HUBBLE
2. GALAXIES
3. SPIRAL
4. GRAVITY
5. DARK MATTER
6. ELLIPTICAL

Page 81

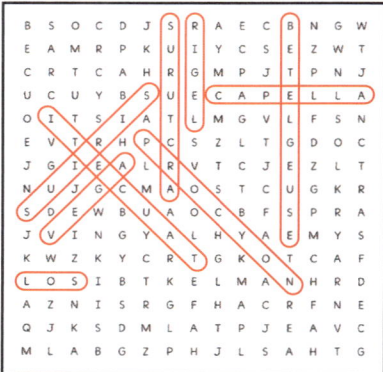

Page 82

1. nucleus
2. Kuiper Belt
3. 4.6
4. two
5. frozen
6. ice

Page 83

Page 84

1. Meteor
2. Shooting Star
3. Meteoroids
4. Comets
5. Asteroids
6. Meteorites

Page 85

Page 89

SPUTNIK

Page 90

1. ENGINE
2. FIREWORKS
3. THRUST
4. SPACECRAFT
5. ROCKETS
6. AERODYNAMIC

Page 92

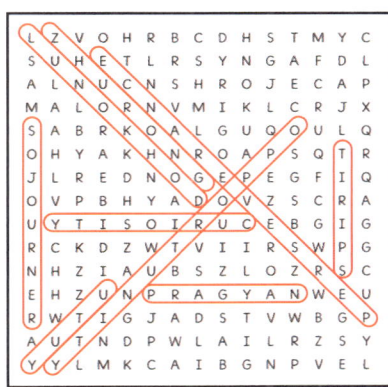

Page 93

Page 96

1. False
2. False
3. True
4. False
5. True
6. True

Page 98

1. Space Race
2. Explorers
3. Space Walks
4. Laika
5. Astronauts

Page 99

Page 101

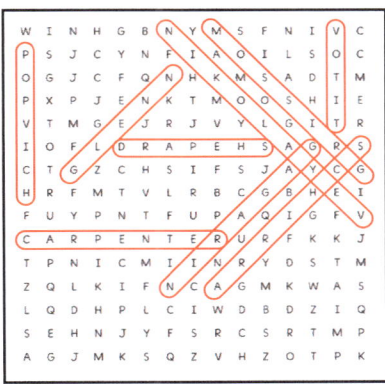

Page 104

1. False
2. True
3. True
4. False
5. True
6. False

Page 105

Page 107

1. NEIL ARMSTRONG
2. ARTEMIS
3. KENNEDY
4. LUNAR GATEWAY
5. BUZZ ALDRIN
6. APOLLO

Page 108

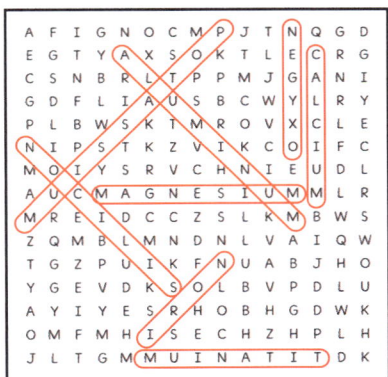

Page 112

1. Telescope
2. Orbit
3. Distant
4. Observatories
5. Hubble
6. Nebulas

Page 113

Page 115

ASTROBIOLOGIST

Page 117

Page 118

1. SPACE TOURIST
2. SPACECRAFT
3. WEIGHTLESSNESS
4. ORBIT
5. PARTICIPANT
6. ASTRONAUTS

About the Author

EMILY GREENHALGH is an award-winning science journalist and the author of *Fun with Oceans and Seas*. Even as a kid, she never met a science fact she didn't like. She grew up in Rhode Island staring into tide pools, flipping over logs to look at bugs, and counting shooting stars in the night sky. Emily trained to become a marine biologist and then a science journalist. Now she helps scientists tell their stories. From climate change and microbes to satellites and exoplanets, Emily loves turning complex science into easy-to-understand ideas. She has worked on commercial fishing boats, tagged sharks, and hiked in Antarctica. In her spare time, she writes speculative fiction, does pottery, and enjoys putting cheese on things. She lives on Cape Cod, Massachusetts, with her husband, their two dogs, and one semi-tolerant cat. Parents, find Emily online at emilygreenhalgh.com.

About the Artist

CANDELA FERRÁNDEZ is a freelance illustrator based in Barcelona, Spain. After studying fine arts at Salamanca University, she earned a postgraduate degree in illustration at EINA (Barcelona). When she was a child, she loved looking for bugs and little animals around gardens. Now she draws them. Children, flowers, plants, and animals define her personal universe, which she also expresses in ceramic pieces. Her illustrations have been published by, among others, Milan Presse, Éditions Larousse, Fleurus, and Penguin Random House, including those in *Fun with 50 States*, *Fun with National Parks*, and *Fun with Oceans and Seas*. Parents, find Candela online at candelaferrandez.com.

Explore the world around you with over a hundred fun activities and cool facts in every BIG book!

MAZES - DOT-TO-DOTS - WORD SEARCHES - COLORING PAGES - CRACK THE CODES - MATCHING GAMES - AND MORE!

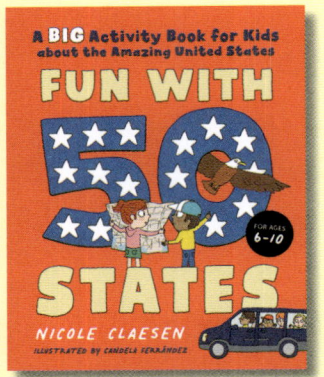

Welcome to the wild and wonderful United States of America!

Learn more about this amazing country, take a virtual trip that reveals hidden attractions, and have fun with activities and wacky facts.

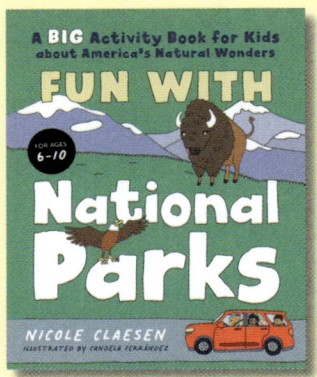

Welcome to America's stunning national parks!

Explore spectacular vistas and delightful surprises in all 63 national parks, including fascinating facts about their landscape, geological features, animals, history, and more.

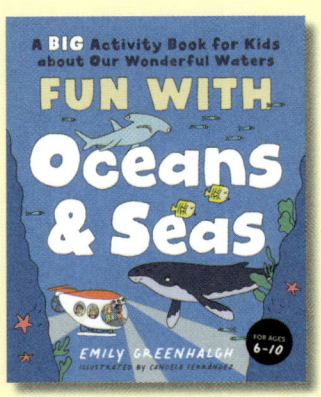

Welcome to the world's wonderful waters!

Dive into the world's magnificent oceans and seas. They're brimming with amazing plants and animals and secrets lurking beneath the surface.

Parents, visit our series page to learn more: bit.ly/458r0Ua

zeitgeistpublishing.com